The Bungalow Journey

A Collection of Poems

DEANNA M. SCOTT

VANN BOOKS

The Bungalow Journey

Published by: VANN BOOKS

First Printing

Library of Congress Control Number: 2016921116
ISBN: 978-0-692-67755-1

Printed in the United States of America

Dedicated to Mom

I walk in your Grace. Thank you.

Table of Contents

The Bungalow Journey

Memories gently arrive on the Bungalow's white porch with its chipped paint.
A dream found inside the wilted rose vine lining the side panel.
Roaring winds shifted summertime honeysuckles, a sweet smell of hope.
Long ago days, I lay outstretched on a soft blanket reading under two oak trees.
Bungalow silence softening the air.

Oh yes, we felt, but we laughed more often.
Resilient with our gifts, the Bungalow had no favorites.

Old worn boots sit at the doorstep.
A rusty clothesline buried into the ground.
Oh, what loveliness it bore.
Blue collar uniforms and cleaning rags floated in the wind.
I picked a plump red tomato from the garden and drank a few sips from the hose.

Days of running across the driveway in my only dress,
Blue and usually stained, I only wore to church and Ms.
Ruth's house,
In exchange for freeze pops and games of connect the dots.

I was eating Ms. Gertie's Fig Newtons and wishing I
stayed for another
Cup of red Kool-Aid.
Mr. Daggi's work truck pulled in the driveway, and I
leaped up for my lollipop
Dangling out his window.
I smiled and ran back to the yard.
What a great day.

I heard the older neighborhood kids laughing in the distance.
My brother and sister, amongst the group, were lucky
To outrun my mother's voice, or I sure would have been
laughing too.
So many days it was just the Bungalow and me.

Now driveways are crossed less often.
Children bring their children to admire and sit with
the Bungalow.
Land still fruitful, wild mushrooms crowd the green
grass, the garden's vegetables
Sprouting sweet and strong.
The old family mailbox lay against the trash can. I prop
it up and take a picture.
The Bungalow Journey continues.

Joy Riddled

Joy riddled with changing season.
Amidst dreams in colors of red.
Riding the stallions till dawn.

Blueberry Lenses

You see me through the wings of a blue angel.
Who you determine me to be.
Is what you say.
Just because you say it,
Don't make it so,
Just because I don't believe it,
Don't make it false.
You love me.
Don't mean we will be together.

Dark Skin Cat

On a blistering summer day, there was a howl in the neighborhood.

There's going to be a gathering at the pond in front of Ms. Ballard's house at one o'clock.

Bored and for no lazy day reason, we watched two cats playing with one another.
A fine calico with a yellow tube top, and a tabby wearing a pink one.
Tomcats anxiously anticipating a peek at some forbidden flesh.
Everybody had money on the calico.
But the tabby learned a few tricks after a few summers down South.
Her meow was low-slung, but her playful bite was created on a gentle night below the moon.

Don't be deceived.

Mama, Mama, the cats are going to scrap.

With one hand in the dish suds, and two feet on the aluminum flooring, Mama leaned out the kitchen window, and said, "Cats will be cats."

Creative Words Fly

Creative words fly to an open heart.
Doubts, clarity, all things captured forever.
Open to love.
Anchored in white heavens dialogue without restraint.
Wishing for rain to wash away the color green.
Memories snuggled away tightly from history.
Spinning a line down in the ocean.
Shreds of love waiting to travel the golden path.
No more dry memories disguised as seconds on the other side of an hour.

Shadows of Butter Bean Blues

Shadows of butter bean blues
Vigilant white tires riding down highways
Pimping sage red bottom pumps
Gathered for unity
Embrace the freedom
Tolerant and with laden,
Rest is near, don't go to sleep.

How Do You Introduce Yourself?

Meeting for the first time
Something you create verbally, sexually, physically.
Introduce our nature to another
Accepting denial of the eye penetration into the aura
Coloring all that circles the heart.
Waking up to a new chance at love.

Alone In Another

Pleasant silence within unveiling love.
The soul is the victor.
If one prefers, you will find all of thee.
Past. Present. Future. Which tune will you compose today?
To hold. To be held. A wish indeed.
Walls dressed with pride.
Stillness familiar and similar to yesterday.
Inhabiting the light of love.
Surrender to the days of tomorrow.
Love not for the faint-hearted or sunlit lucidity.
Stirring faith and wonder of an offer to open my heart.
The dance of accepting desirable love conditions commence.
Be gentle.

It's Okay

Isn't it always okay?
Doesn't it always work out?
I'm still breathing, so that means I have another chance.
No matter how hard.
No matter if no one says you can do it.
It will be okay.
It will.
You can't let go.
You can't turn back.
You will make it.
But you still have to take a step.
You just don't know.
Does it matter what people say?
You have this feeling.
It's in your stomach, in your shoulders, gripping you,
pulling you. Saying, "Be patient."
Saying, "Wait."
Saying, "It's going to happen."

But you have to sit.
You have to be still.
Patience.

Love Flows into My Life in Endless Streams

A Coca-Cola, a little smoke and a snack.
Neighbors impede at the corner on
A chilly fall, a few before-winter days.
Nippy enough but warmer still.
Three ladies at the corner of Kayak and Aquinas Ave.
Hands on hips, 1 fair 2 not.
The politician did not win.
Everyone is stunned. What will we do that we didn't do
anyways last year?
School buses throttle the engine. Children scattering
and climb aboard structure.
Stretching limbs, ideas dancing within the smoke circles
as I sit watching out the window.
Peace and quiet within silence.
Reality a distant second off a 23-hour clock stuck at
10:31 am or pm. Depending on the mood.
Freedom days sliding by.

Uncross the left leg from the right. Cross the right leg over the left.
A lone brown leaf singed with rust dangles on the sandy brown tree.
Refusing to fall. Refusing to let go as all others.
The wind blows a soft whisper toward the beat.
The leaf still holding on.
Refusing to surrender until I turn away.
I appease.
I drink a little Coca-Cola, smoke a little smoke, and grab a snack.

Hair Razzle Dazzle

Delighted by a memory of yesterday.
A footing of wealth launching dawn.
School house blues and summer time follies with the
lineage afar.
Old brown desk amidst a shrine of cobwebs.
Hair razzle dazzle.
Mismatched socks and candy-colored frocks.
This is such, the such.
Proud with love surrendering while adding one plus one.
Oh no.
Burgundy mirrors are shining when light is bestowed on
The veiled stars.

Space

The illusion of space
Needing to separate thyself from another self
Comfortable in the words that are spoken
Mirror of behaviors once held but a minute ago
Responsive or changing but of acceptance
Holding love
That will teach you to love me
The right way
My way.
Is it my way of loving
Or a mere resemblance of a distant past?
Love. Love. Love.
Accepting love. Seeking love. Speaking love. Feeling love.
How do I love myself in another?
Understanding in order to proceed together
Togetherness has a destination date.
Or is it done when it's done?
Love will banter with the gentle lover.

Foxhole

Dearth under the foxhole.
Assurances of ask and it is given.
Realism of finding a way home.
Anticipation in the sky.
Fretfulness on the soil.
While lost in the middle of delight.
Running to the sun.
A life delighted in many to be forever.
I know how and too similar to not be.
Spoken another way.
Erstwhile routes are my birth.
An odd voice must persist,
Too much to do.
But there is a choice.
Do it.

Freedom

Seeking truth in mysterious seawaters
Obscuring in refreshing air
Cherry-picking clarity above bewilderment
Inner rampant courage with no terminus
Love in the midst of change
Desire the soul which chooses you
Offer silence during intellectual threats
Freedom is a soul ballad.

Mist in the Distance

Mist in the distance on a
Cold morning walk.
Allowing new thoughts to deliver creative light.
Disarming old record players
Seeking help
Losing confusion
Love no more
Trust less ish
Rush to meet destiny
Along the tracks of earth
No destination to love
Tender sweet highs.

All My Life I Have Avoided Goodbyes

Such wisdom. Such womanhood. All facets of colors.
Soaring with the blue-gray birds in the sky during a crisp fall day.
The illusion of gap is losing its strength in my mind.
The cement bleachers have lost their appeal in the common areas.
I'm coming. Please wait for me.
I have something to say during this time of light.
Before you envision the other side, stand still.
I know it's selfish. I took my good ole time coming up the road,
Please forgive me.
Daring to dream of crossing over the threshold.
No longer sleeping in the day.
Silently, waiting, just to watch who to wait for.
I'm awake. I'm not sleeping any more.

Yellow Beans and Green Beans

I wrote a memory from a distance
When I arrived at the origination no words formed
Separation provided with a far grander scene of happiness
Origination served no purpose
Feeling for optimistic love
Travel deep into the woods
Sounds alive with passion
Searching for the beat to hear my tune
Faintness of awareness crosses my path
Dead leaves gently descend from the withered trees
Holding the key to my future
Yellow beans and green beans grow just fine together

Move

Go this way.
No, go that way.
Hopeful about the choice.
Right or wrong.
Move.

The Trail

Days spent in phantasms,
Too delicious to flavor warm sun on an unexpected
winter day.
The sun lusters through fragmented foliage.

I pulled out a bologna and cheese sandwich sitting on
lavender tree stumps,
What a delightful time.

Serenading to Mother Nature on a 9-mile slog.
Messages from the earth, guiding me, to awaken to the
glorious now.

Heart racing, no end in sight
Out of darkness a white-tailed buck dashing onto the trail
Signaling the way home.
Racing to signs of where to next.
Visualizing the future.

Arriving at another destination.
But within walking distance of my dreams.

Are We Healing To Live Or To Die?

Life was on cruise control
My words come with honest feelings.
My hurt doesn't want to land upside nobody's head.
Logic has no place in an upside-down world.
Preach, teach, reach for all that you know and deliver it
within a time frame a person needs and you will forever
die one day at a time, so you say.
Have you ever been driven down a highway with no car?

Sightseer

Sightseer in a circle of light
Isolated within the love of my nature
Only you
Nightfall edging the willows
I bellow to see
Centuries spent off in the reserve
Free heart chakra
Fences made of purple miasma
Only you see all

Max

One hot smoldering night,
Max lay beneath the divan, stretching out his aged body.
Triple-stick candle scenting the air with clean linen.
Television numbing the mind
Purposely distracting night worries.
Yellow daisies on the end table.
Initiation rising.
Max licks and laps at an old wound under strengthened fur.
He was the kindest dog I've never owned.

Rise Once More

Climb once again
The sun has shiny bright glare
Evolve your mind in grace
Release the grasp of yesterday.
Root your forthcoming with courage
Seek your difference
Die no more.

Poem

Essential woman of the world.
Exiled truth
Spiritual lessons are every fiber of life.
Cement mingling in trust.
Heart rhythm of patience.
How to kiss the sun on a Monday morning?

Captivated mind
Dangling within a jig at night.
Laughing, dancing and prancing
Happiness, laughter and all that jazz.
Open your door and let in life.
Close the window and free your spirit.
So many to dance, are you sure?
Jig here, jig there
Feminine air
Open your mind and free yourself.

Tit for tat
Tat for tit

DeAnna M. Scott

Beauty Is Intriguing

Beauty is enchanting to the absent nature at dusk.
An attempt to cuckold the eye, my heart beat as your chaperon.
Delight with my soul.
Common love and a trace of warm cinnamon dew.
Wakefulness no more.
Seek to discover the worth of verses.
Shift towards a gentle vibration.
An offer of quiet contemplation among the masses.
Observer walking inside the valley,
Light my path to forgiveness.
Open my heart.
Open my eyes.
Relinquish my savior to lemon drop dreams.
Weary ones be no more.
Softly influence my imagination as
I walk in peace.
Dreaming forgoes to awaken in purpose.

After Work

Tender, supping tomatoes tilting with grace.
Budding rose petals preamble the beat of earth's
quiet melodies.
Broken-legged crickets chirp off beat.
Tree birds' tweet to their young, prancing around full
of wiggly white worms.

Four-legged panting dogs released from their dwelling,
hauling their master down fissured sidewalks.
Yellow lanterns shower light along the carefully paved
driveways beckoning to
Car lights driving eagerly into the distance of nowhere
and everywhere.

Home.

Dishes clanking. Pots singing a warm tune primed for
sustenance.

Jazz ringing in the background of a sunset.
Bustling horns, whispering flutist and overdue toe taps.
A glorious day.

Mirror Images

Existing in this creation as self, all else is commencing, as the journey begins towards grace.

Twinkling stars will recur, but fall short of distress.

All one, it is me, and will be forever you, no matter what we do, or how everyone does it.

Serenading the energy of passion, while joyriding in a chocolate rollercoaster.

Time is.

No ending or beginning.

Enlightenment to all questions,

One true answer, the exception, always love another.

Love amity lies at the core of the heart.

While reassessing a lost vision, magically, the world opens to an individual voice.

Withholding thy own motives, safely protected from the paranoia of suffering.

Each moment is a glorious day, which shall never be again.

Solace of the Moon

Laughing her way to freedom,
All the days of her life.
Within the soul.
Never mentioning the truth of it all,
Solace has no moon,
Nor does it bite at the wings of light.
It does not matter who was wrong,
It is only about the truth of right.
Noting it all down within the membranes of shoelaces,
Walking the path of our heart.
Your heart.
My heart.
Beating the soul of you,
Healing within the light,
Basking in the light.
Something has to rain on the window of love,
You are a masterpiece of art,
Sing the highest tune,
Paint the biggest picture,
Love the open heart.

I Give You a Reason to Love Me

So, the lesson I learned
Was the lesson I taught.
Loved someone more than myself and watching them
stay forever.
The circle is complete.
I gave you a reason to love you.
And that shall always be.
You give me a reason to love me.
And that is that.

Miracles

Silently waiting, striving to create a world that does
not resemble
Yesterday.
Staying present.
Dipping in and out of awareness,
How my thoughts are creating tomorrow.
Spotting coincidences, left by angels.
Tasting delicious miracles.
Life is as it should be.
Magical.

Don't Fix

The mosquitoes are quite bothersome this Georgia summer,
Destination truly unknown.
We seek solitude with a blast of flavor.
Quiet teas at a counter, soaking up knowledge from fellow
souls to see how they are coming along in their journey.
I dabbled a little, or some may say splashed a lot, in the
circle of healing and remain indifferent to it all.
So healed is placed on the shelf for later deliberation, if
anyone cares to ask.
I see no need for its existence at this place and time.
Old stuff, again no author, so I relinquish publishing rights.
I've invested 100 percent but not all at once, only
down payments.
I yearn for a new voice, a new sound and feel to categorize
all my current logic.
Boredom is but a dilemma and not a friend of the
hoax patience.
So, see beyond the words and feel the letters.
It's a practice I've mastered without knowledge.

So, I unstiffen to allow you into my heart and not just my mind, which is a place of its own, and will have you lost amongst ideas and understandings that are sometimes confused with wisdom and love.

Verses have no true destination, sometimes only meant for the whiteness of paper.

A way to place a thought into a feeling into a dilemma and explain chaos or soothe gentleness, no matter its destination, it is the intent of the reader, which will always claim the prize.

Although readings will be done, it is subject to the writer and never to be judged how it is received or when it is received, it must be released, which is the importance of patience.

The broken heart will mend, the mind will heal, the blessed will be assured, the listener will lead, but it will not release the notion to know more, only to want less.

Clarity is an issue of vision.

It is not the mind that issues clarity, it is within the heart.

All will be seen when ready.

Nothing is ever held from you, but it will protect you from the essence of its truth if that's what you so desire.

No one will ever be able to put a finger on the words of hurt or pain.

It is only for you to put a soft touch on the experience you so desire.

Live beloved, with an open heart.

Surrender

Surrender is as all things of the universe
An illusion of strength that exists only in the strong-minded
But all so comforting
To a soul that has been watched over and kept close to
the bosom
Thinking of all I am to be and already am
Feeling so distant from its cradle
I can imagine feeling so good.
My heartbeat flutters and rises to a new temptation that
is more delightful than all freedom of self
Dropping mystery and delusion of healing and distance
All is really required is a present shift in sight
A sudden tremor of chills running down your arms to
know truth
Passion will always be passion but as if to never have felt
the wind howls embrace.

Garden Day

One glorious day amongst flora.
Rifling for passion in the vegetable garden.
Chili peppers sweltering within my hand,
Bowed over, posterior screaming gratitude while
harvesting.
Patiently dipped and lapped in vinegar boil,
Then incrusted in a frosty sack.
Positioned in a cold case to
Rise again during the changing seasons
Stews serviced with servitude.
Emptiness be no more.
Soil nourishment meshed in the now.

Yellow Beans

Revisiting a distant memory
Dusk was upon us when the beast showed its shadowy face
No words formed
Distance provides a far grander scene than reality of
struggles and happiness
Origination served no purpose
Feeling abandoned for survivors
Travel deep into the woods
Vibrations alive with passion
Searching for the beat
To write my tune
Faint smell of awareness crosses my path
Dead leaves gently descend from the withered trees
Holding the key to my future
Refuse to release the grip of my ego
Yellow beans and green beans grow just fine together

Love Is History

Love is a narration of noble reminders.
Resting upon hinged decrees, continuing to smile at dawn.
Sunshine so warm and kind belonging to me.
Love is history of good feelings along the river banks.
Silver coins shining on crashing waves.
Heart murmuring a soft song inside sea shells.
Unimaginable thoughts of ecstasy.
Kind words whispered into the dusk.

Banana Moon

My love, I will forever search the softness of lips meshed
gently on a blackberry pancake.
Hair radiant and dark, glistening with soft gold beads.
Searching for the light within the seam of thread.
Within the gates of love.

Your Destiny Your Right

Alas, the night has come,
Gently steeping amongst the stars.
Casting a new moon with infinite promises.
Dream anew. All that I have is gained at once.
Feeling no more is less of a burden.
Searching to rise within the furrows.
Sought after by many, each revealing a way to surrender.
Accepting to gift the soul of its past.
Withholding amid the pressure of the novel
Rising within the wings of wealth.
Rise and take place amongst your peers.
Your call.
Our right.

Healing in My Mother's Garden

Healing in my mother's garden.
Donning a pair of worn tennis shoes, one size too big.
Pallid tube socks trekked to my knees, safeguarding my
ankles from masticating red ants and deer ticks rifling
for skin to suckle.
I stepped out onto the red stained porch which held a
brown woven basket waiting to be filled with vegetable
treasures.

"You better put a hat on your head," my mother cautioned.

I concurred, and leapt off the porch with elation, hatless.

Red ripened tomatoes, chili peppers, jalapeno peppers,
and yellow beans mixed with green beans, and a few
small watermelons welcomed me on a hot scorching
July afternoon.

Rabbits scuttling gingerly about the flank, whopping
bellies from feasting, curiously gazing at the stranger
donned in such silly apparel.

Nostalgia was the first-picked vegetable of the day.
Remembering lost yesterdays spent in the city.
Foreign memories of hard work, long days and a non-
existent harvest.

I was finally home. A place no worries could penetrate.
A lost soul reaching for dreams, wondering if just out
of touch with reality,
I plucked a few tomatoes hanging low on the vine.
I thought about my grandparents, who were farmers as
I soiled my hands in the earth.
My lower back singed as I bent over the harvest.

My crown chakra began to tingle as the sun penetrated
beneath my black locks.
I delighted in the natural vitamin D.

Crops will rise, bear fruit, die and start again.